BEAVERS

LIVING WILD

Published by Creative Education
P.O. Box 227, Mankato, Minnesota 56002
Creative Education is an imprint of The Creative Company
www.thecreativecompany.us

Design and production by Mary Herrmann
Art direction by Rita Marshall
Printed in the United States of America

Photographs by Alamy (AF archive, Juniors Bildarchiv GmbH, Robert McGouey/Wildlife, Prisma Bildagentur AG), Dreamstime (Fallsview, Gail Johnson, Joycemarrero, Viktor Krajnyik, Maunger, Jeff Whyte), Getty Images (TOM MCHUGH, Sven Zacek), iStockphoto (cascoly, ericfoltz, imagegrafx, Little_Things, Lynn_Bystrom, photographer3431, raclro, Terryfic3D, webmink), Shutterstock (belizar, BMJ, dan_nurgitz, Bill Frische, Jason Kasumovic, kojihirano, KOO, Hugh Lansdown, Brian Lasenby, oksana.perkins, outdoorsman, Pictureguy, VLADJ55), Wikipedia (Adam Cuerden, Daderot, Kürschner, Oregon State Beavers)

Library of Congress Cataloging-in-Publication Data
Gish, Melissa.
Beavers / Melissa Gish.
p. cm. — (Living wild)
Includes bibliographical references and index.
Summary: A scientific look at beavers, including their habitats, physical characteristics such as their gnawing teeth, behaviors, relationships with humans, and abundance of the rodents in the world today.
ISBN 978-1-60818-414-9
1. Beavers—Juvenile literature. I. Title. II. Series: Living wild.

QL737.R632.G57 2014
599.37—dc23   2013031814

CCSS: RI.5.1, 2, 3, 8; RST.6-8.1, 2, 5, 6, 8; RH.6-8.3, 4, 5, 6, 7, 8

First Edition
9 8 7 6 5 4 3 2 1

CREATIVE EDUCATION

BEAVERS

Melissa Gish

A pair of beavers is hard at work beside a creek in

western Oregon's Umpqua National Forest.

A pair of beavers is hard at work beside a creek. In western Oregon's Umpqua National Forest, a resurgence of willow trees has drawn the beavers back to their ancestral home after a six-decade absence. At the creek's edge, the female scoops up thick mud and leaves, pressing the mass against her chest with her front paws as she trudges up the bank. Not far from her, the male gnaws on the trunk of a willow, pausing every few bites to listen for the creaking or snapping sounds that will tell him that the tree will fall. Soon, the tree crashes to the ground! The female hurries to help her mate strip the tree of its branches and chew the trunk into logs that can be rolled to the creek. There the pair will build a dam to create a pond—the perfect place to make a home and raise a family.

WHERE IN THE WORLD THEY LIVE

The two beaver species are found in North America, Europe, and Asia. Chinese and Mongolian populations are especially lean, but the animals are abundant throughout their North American range. The colored dots represent some common locations of the two species.

■ **North American Beaver**
northern Canada to northern Mexico

■ **Eurasian Beaver**
Europe, Russia, China, Mongolia

CREATURE OF LAND AND WATER

North American beavers and Eurasian beavers are the two species in the Castoridae family. The Old English word *beofor* and the Old French word *bièvre* referred to Eurasian beavers as far back as the 9th century A.D. When Europeans first traveled to the Americas, the word "beaver" was used to describe these fur-bearing rodents, which hunters and trappers found in abundance. Known for the sharp front teeth they use for gnawing wood, beavers are related to other small **mammals** that gnaw, such as mice, marmots, and ground squirrels. Beavers are **semiaquatic** mammals that live in riparian zones, or forested areas next to rivers, streams, or lakes. North American beavers can be found throughout the continent, from northern Canada to northern Mexico. Although Eurasian beavers were hunted to **extinction** in many countries in the 18th and 19th centuries, they continue to inhabit more than 30 countries in Europe, from northern Finland to northern Spain and eastward into Russia and parts of China and Mongolia.

Male and female beavers look alike. They can grow to 70 pounds (31.8 kg), though the average weight is between

Eurasian and North American beavers are not genetically compatible to be able to mate with each other.

The Eurasian beaver is the largest rodent in its native habitats of Europe and Asia.

30 and 60 pounds (13.6–27.2 kg). At 35 to 40 inches (88.9–102 cm) long—which includes a 12-inch (30.5 cm) tail—the North American beaver is the largest rodent in North America and the second-largest rodent in the world, after the 100-pound (45.4 kg) capybara of South America. The Eurasian beaver is about the same size as the North American beaver, but its physical appearance is different in a number of ways.

Eurasian beavers have narrower, less oval-shaped tails than North American beavers as well as smaller skulls. Also, because they have slightly shorter legs than North American beavers, Eurasian beavers are less capable of walking on their hind legs—something North American beavers tend to do over short distances. Eurasian beavers have triangular nasal openings, while North American beavers' are square. Most Eurasian beavers are beige or reddish, but North American beavers have greater variation in their coat colors, from light brown to black.

The beaver's front paws, each sporting five slender, clawed digits, are like **dexterous** hands. The back paws have five long, clawed toes with flexible skin webbing between them. The hind paws are used like flippers to

Beavers sleep on the water to protect themselves from predators, even before they are finished building a home.

A beaver's tail functions as a rudder to help the animal steer, or change direction, while swimming.

propel the beaver while swimming. The claw on the second toe of each hind foot is split and is called a comb claw. A beaver runs these claws through its two layers of fur in a circular motion to lift out embedded dirt and debris from its coat. Stiff guard hairs can be up to 2.4 inches (6.1 cm) long, and soft, woolly underfur grows to only half that length. Beavers spend a great deal of time grooming and waterproofing their fur by cleaning it and coating the guard hairs with an oil secreted from **glands** near the tail. The beaver's dense fur keeps the animal warm and its skin dry when underwater. Also, the slick, oily coating helps beavers float and protects them from their enemies' bites and scratches. A layer of fat insulating the beaver's vital organs from extreme temperatures is another protective feature of a beaver's body.

Like many semiaquatic animals, such as hippopotamuses and alligators, beavers' eyes, ears, and nostrils are situated on the top of the head so that they remain above water when beavers swim. Beavers can hold their breath underwater for up to 15 minutes, though 5- to 6-minute dives are most common. While diving, the beaver's heart rate slows down to about half its normal rate to conserve oxygen in the blood. When beavers dive, muscles in the nostrils and ears pinch shut, and nictitating (*NIK-tih-tate-ing*) membranes (see-through inner eyelids) protect the eyes from debris. Special fur-lined inner lips close behind the front teeth, and a wide tongue blocks the throat, allowing beavers to gnaw trees underwater without drowning.

A beaver's skull is thicker than that of other rodents, as it must absorb the force of chomping large trees. Sixteen

An acute sense of smell helps beavers avoid areas in which predators have left scent trails.

Beavers can swim about five miles (8 km) per hour and swim completely submerged for about a half mile (0.8 km).

A type of snowshoe, a cactus species, and a Canadian pastry also share the shape and name of a beaver's tail.

Beaver teeth are protected by a hard, orange enamel on the front and have a soft back that wears more slowly.

grinding molars fill the back of the beaver's upper and lower jaws, while the front teeth—four chisel-shaped, deeply rooted incisors—grow continuously throughout the beaver's life and are worn down by chewing wood. A beaver's strong lower jaw muscles provide chainsaw-like power for cutting through trees. A beaver can chew through a tree 6 inches (15.2 cm) thick in 15 minutes.

The beaver's most distinctive characteristic is its tail, which is flat and covered with black, scaly skin. Beavers lean on their tails while cutting trees or reaching food. Tails act as rudders that help beavers maneuver while diving and swimming. The tail also serves as a storage tank for fat reserves. While beavers' eyesight and hearing are not considered strong, their sense of smell is acute. Because they are most active at dawn, dusk, and at night, beavers rely on smell to detect predators and select food in dim light. Scent is also used in communication. The beaver's urine is stored in a pair of castor sacs located under the skin near the base of the tail and is concentrated into a strong-smelling substance called castoreum, which is secreted to mark territory and attract mates.

Because beavers tend to remain close to water sources

Only the upper and lower incisors (the four teeth at the front of the mouth) are coated with orange enamel.

Black bears dig into beaver lodges in springtime when the bears are hungriest and the lodges are weakest.

and can hide in the mud-and-stick homes they build in the water, they can often avoid predators. However, because they move slowly, once a black bear or cougar targets them, escape is difficult. Typically, only when larger prey such as moose and deer are scarce will wolves attack beavers that venture onto land, which occurs most often in fall and early spring, when beavers travel away from their watery habitats in search of food.

Coyotes attack beavers frequently, and, in many mountainous habitats, beavers and deer make up the bulk of coyotes' diets. Although beavers generally avoid inhabiting alligator-infested waters, researchers have observed alligators encountering and preying on beavers. The beaver's greatest enemy is humans, though. Creating dams that reduce or eliminate flowing water and cutting down the trees that beavers need to survive are actions that have affected beaver populations in both North America and in Europe. In addition, many beavers are killed because humans find their activities around waterways and farms disruptive, and since beavers are considered an abundant species, they are vulnerable to seasonal hunting and trapping.

The practice of stretching and drying beaver pelts on round hoops or boards for 7 to 10 days is still used today.

During the summer months, beavers feast on soft aquatic plants as well as tender new pine needles.

Despite having teeth and a lower jaw powerful enough to chew through bone, beavers do not eat other animals. They are herbivores, surviving solely on woody vegetation and aquatic plants. Beavers eat bark and wood from any kind of tree, though they prefer aspen, poplar, willow, birch, cottonwood, and alder, as these trees have relatively soft bark. Beavers will also eat grasslike plants such as cattails, rushes, and sedges as well as water lilies upon availability.

Once a beaver chooses its mate for life, the pair claims a territory. Beavers live in family groups called colonies, which are made up of 4 to 12 members consisting of parents and offspring from 2 breeding seasons. Beavers make their homes where water flows and trees are abundant, altering their habitats to suit their needs. They can construct dams that turn even the smallest trickling stream into a deep pond. This will provide them with protection from predators and allow them to store food for the winter. Beavers require a pond that is four to six feet (1.2–1.8 m) deep.

To begin construction of a dam, beavers must first divert slowly flowing water so that the dam will not be

If a beaver is frightened away while chewing a tree, it may not return to the tree until the following year.

Beavers typically select trees up to 12 inches (30.5 cm) thick but may topple trees twice this size to eat the bark.

Fish in dammed beaver ponds are often larger than fish in other ponds because they get more food.

washed away before it is completed. They do this by piling rocks along the path of the stream to slow the water and send it in a new direction. Beavers can carry rocks using one or both front paws while walking on three legs or on just their back legs, supported by their tail.

Then beavers look for something such as a rock outcropping or a large tree stump on which to anchor the dam where the flowing water is shallowest. In slow-moving water, the dam is typically straight across from bank to bank, but in faster-flowing water, the dam must be curved inward to ease the water pressure against it. The base of the dam is constructed of branches and logs buried

upright like fence posts in the mud of the streambed.
Then the wall is formed with carefully fitted materials
that range from rocks and logs to plant matter and mussel
shells, all packed together with mud, leaves, and grass.
Beavers will put anything useful into their dams—even
debris such as abandoned camping equipment or the
bones of dead animals.

Trees that once stood on the land around the stream
become submerged, making them easy for beavers to
access. In addition, beavers often cut trenches in the land
surrounding the pond. These canals fill with water, so
beavers can swim to reach distant trees, cut them down,

By plugging its throat with its wide tongue, a beaver can tow branches through the water without drowning.

and float them back to the pond, where they are stored underwater for consumption throughout the winter or used in the construction of the beaver's home.

Once the dam is completed, the area behind the dam fills with water. Beavers may create spillways in a dam to release some of the pond water so that it does not get too high and destroy the dam. On average, beaver dams are 6 feet (1.8 m) high, 15 feet (4.6 m) wide, and 5 feet (1.5 m) thick. Dams are maintained and repaired as necessary, and beavers may continue to add to dams over many years, making them much bigger and stronger. The

longest beaver dam on record was first photographed by a National Aeronautics and Space Administration (NASA) **satellite** in 1990 and reconfirmed as recently as 2010. Located in Wood Buffalo National Park in the Canadian province of Alberta, the dam is 2,790 feet (850 m) long. Researchers estimate the dam is more than 30 years old.

Two types of beaver homes are built of the same materials and with the same techniques used in dam construction. One type of home, a bank den, is dug into the side of a bank and covered with branches, mud, and leaves. Bank dens, which have a single room, are built on rivers that are large or that move swiftly. Ponds and lakes are where beavers build multi-room lodges. Domed lodges have an opening in the top for ventilation and underwater access to the inside. The first room, or chamber, built just above the water line, is where beavers dry off after entering the lodge. The second chamber is built above the first chamber, like the second story of a house. This is where beavers sleep and care for their young, called kits.

Because beavers mate for life, if one partner dies, the other will usually remain single or find another mate.

Beavers can often be observed using their front paws to roll up lily pads like burritos before eating them.

Beaver kits play to strengthen their muscles and learn social behaviors that will help them work together as adults.

Because young kits tire easily when swimming, they may climb onto their mother's back for a ride around their pond.

Beavers reach maturity when they are about two and a half years old. In southern climates, mating takes place from November to March, while beavers in northern climates mate from January to March. After a **gestation** period of 100 to 110 days, up to 9 kits are born. (Four is the most commonly sized litter, though.) Newborns weigh 8 to 24 ounces (227–680 g), and unlike many small mammals such as skunks and badgers, which are born blind and hairless, beaver kits are born with their eyes open. They also have fur and visible front teeth. Kits are able to swim within a day after birth.

Mother beavers feed their offspring milk for up to three months. The milk produced by a female beaver is some of the richest milk of all mammals. Its high fat and protein content helps young beavers quickly develop the layer of fat they will need in order to survive in their aquatic environment. Within two to three weeks, beaver kits begin eating leaves and twigs in addition to milk, and by three months of age they are fully **weaned**.

Offspring from the previous year remain with the family and help care for the new kits, cleaning and grooming them, carrying their waste out of the lodge, and bringing

fresh leaf litter into the lodge for bedding. Beavers are born with gnawing and basic construction instincts, but they learn engineering techniques from watching their parents and older siblings. When beavers are about two and a half years old, they leave the family and go off in search of mates and territories of their own. Beavers can live more than 20 years. Depending on the size of a pond or lake, several generations of beaver families may establish their own territories within the area. However, beavers that are not family members are chased away.

The bond between a mother and her offspring can last for many years— even over several generations.

The figure at the top of a Pacific Northwest tribe's totem pole was given the ultimate respect and admiration.

BUILDING A BEAVER EMPIRE

No other animal has had greater influence on North American history than the beaver. In fact, it was one of the major reasons Europeans **colonized** the vast reaches of North America, from northern Canada to the Gulf of Mexico. On a quest for spices from Asia, explorers encountered the New World, but finding no spices, the Europeans of the late 1600s and early 1700s turned their attention to another commodity that became even more valuable: beaver **pelts**.

Having overhunted beavers nearly to extinction in Europe, British and French traders flooded North America, trapping beavers and trading for pelts with American Indians. Trappers and traders sent millions of beaver pelts to European hatters (hat makers). In a process called felting, the beaver fur was shaved short, soaked in a chemical solution, and then dried to create a soft fabric. This was then stretched over wooden blocks to form top hats.

Beaver pelts became so valuable that British and French governments fought wars to control the fur trade. In 1670, the British government formed the Hudson's Bay Company to be the exclusive trader in the region surrounding

The Hudson's Bay Company issued special paper currency as well as marked coins to pay for beaver pelts.

Many American Indians called the beaver the "sacred center of the land" for its ability to create healthy habitats.

This stamp commemorates the endangered Mongolian beaver, a Eurasian subspecies found only in Mongolia's Wulungu River.

northern Canada's Hudson Bay. The Hudson's Bay Company traded everything from stockings and fishhooks to tobacco and guns for beaver pelts. One beaver pelt would buy a man 2 shirts, and 10 pelts would buy him a gun. At the height of the trading era, between 1853 and 1877, the Hudson's Bay Company sold nearly 3 million pelts to England for about $6 each, or $167 by today's standards. During this time, a beaver trapper may have earned $50,000 in one year—equivalent to $1.4 million today.

By the 1900s, the popularity of silk reduced the demand for beaver pelts, allowing beaver populations in both Europe and North America to rebound. The animal continued to have symbolic importance, though. Since its 1851 appearance on Canada's first postage stamp, the "Three Penny Beaver," the beaver has been featured on seven other Canadian stamps. The beaver has adorned the Canadian nickel since 1937, and in 1975, the beaver became Canada's official national animal. In 2006, Canada minted the world's first square coin. The gold-plated $3 collector coin commemorating the history of the British fur trade features Queen Elizabeth II on the front and a beaver on the back.

In the United States, the beaver was selected to represent two states (New York and Oregon) in a 1987 set of 22-cent stamps featuring wildlife from all 50 states. The Eurasian beaver appeared on a Swedish postage stamp in 1996 and on a Russian silver coin in 2008 as well as on stamps from Russia, Germany, and France. Eurasian beavers also appeared on a set of four stamps in Mongolia in 1989, where the species' population has declined dramatically.

Long before beavers had monetary value, they held artistic and social value to many native **cultures**. Most American Indian tribes revered beavers and thought they possessed magical powers. In the **mythology** of the Delaware and Wyandot Indians of southeastern Canada

In 1678, the Hudson's Bay Company designed its official symbol to feature four beavers and two moose.

FROM "THE HUNTING OF THE SNARK"

"Just the place for a Snark!" the Bellman cried,
   As he landed his crew with care;
Supporting each man on the top of the tide
   By a finger entwined in his hair.

"Just the place for a Snark! I have said it twice:
   That alone should encourage the crew.
Just the place for a Snark! I have said it thrice:
   What I tell you three times is true."

The crew was complete: it included a Boots—
   A maker of Bonnets and Hoods—
A Barrister, brought to arrange their disputes—
   And a Broker, to value their goods.

A Billiard-marker, whose skill was immense,
   Might perhaps have won more than his share—
But a Banker, engaged at enormous expense,
   Had the whole of their cash in his care.

There was also a Beaver, that paced on the deck,
   Or would sit making lace in the bow:
And had often (the Bellman said) saved them from wreck,
   Though none of the sailors knew how....

The last of the crew needs especial remark,
   Though he looked an incredible dunce:
He had just one idea—but, that one being "Snark,"
   The good Bellman engaged him at once.

He came as a Butcher: but gravely declared,
   When the ship had been sailing a week,
He could only kill Beavers. The Bellman looked scared,
   And was almost too frightened to speak:

But at length he explained, in a tremulous tone,
   There was only one Beaver on board;
And that was a tame one he had of his own,
   Whose death would be deeply deplored.

The Beaver, who happened to hear the remark,
   Protested, with tears in its eyes,
That not even the rapture of hunting the Snark
   Could atone for that dismal surprise!...

The Beaver's best course was, no doubt, to procure
   A second-hand dagger-proof coat—
So the Baker advised it—and next, to insure
   Its life in some Office of note:

This the Banker suggested, and offered for hire
   (On moderate terms), or for sale,
Two excellent Policies, one Against Fire,
   And one Against Damage From Hail.

Yet still, ever after that sorrowful day,
   Whenever the Butcher was by,
The Beaver kept looking the opposite way,
   And appeared unaccountably shy.

by Lewis Carroll (1832–98)

and the northeastern U.S., the beaver is the creator of the world. Other tribes feature beavers in different roles.

A Seminole legend tells that long ago, beavers lived in Florida and Georgia's Okefenokee Swamp. People kidnapped beaver kits from the swamp to raise as pets. The king of the beavers promised to do anything, if only the people would stop taking the kits. The people wanted dams to drain the swamp and make farmland, so the beavers built them many dams. But soon the people forgot their agreement and began kidnapping beaver kits again. Upset, the beavers chewed through the dams, stopping one bite short of making a hole that would let all the water rush through. When the people next came to kidnap kits, the beaver king slapped his tail on the water's surface, and all the beavers gave their dams one last chomp. The dams broke, and Okefenokee Swamp was flooded once more. To this day, when beavers spot people around their homes, they slap their tails on the water in warning and then dive underwater to escape the danger.

According to an Ojibwe legend, Beaver once had a beautiful, bushy tail, but he was boastful and tried to make Woodpecker jealous. But Woodpecker preferred his own

When food is scarce, beavers will eat their own fecal pellets to gain nutrients from the plant fiber contained in them.

tail, which helped him balance as he pecked on trees. Beaver asked Muskrat if Muskrat wished he had a tail like Beaver's. But Muskrat liked his own tail, too, which helped him steer while swimming. Beaver then called out to Rattlesnake, "Don't you wish you had a bushy tail like mine?" But Rattlesnake liked having a tail that could make noise to warn of danger. Beaver was so angry that no one made a fuss about his tail that he got distracted while cutting down a tree. When the tree fell, it landed on Beaver's tail, flattening it. Beaver was sad, but Woodpecker explained how Beaver's tail was now strong enough to provide balance while cutting trees. Muskrat admired Beaver's flat tail because it could now help him steer while swimming. And Rattlesnake was pleased with how Beaver could now slap his tail on the water to warn of danger. This convinced Beaver that now he had the best tail of all the animals.

In literature, a beaver character created by American author and conservationist Thornton Burgess is featured in the 1917 novel *The Adventures of Paddy the Beaver*. Burgess wrote more than 170 books in his lifetime—many about animals such as Paddy the Beaver—to teach lessons about the values of friendship and sharing. More contemporary

characters are Ace and Bub, the Flying Beaver Brothers, who star in a series of graphic novels by Maxwell Eaton III. The first two books, *The Flying Beaver Brothers and the Evil Penguin Plan* and *The Flying Beaver Brothers and the Fishy Business*, were published in 2012.

The beaver's engineering aptitude has made it a natural fit as the mascot for both the Massachusetts Institute of Technology (MIT) and the California Institute of Technology (Caltech). Other schools, such as Canada's Huron University College and the University of Toronto; Minnesota's Bemidji State University; and Oregon State University all promote planning and hard work through their beaver mascots. The symbol of Parks Canada, the Canadian parks and landmarks agency, is also a beaver.

Reilly (far left) and his beaver crew helped other forest animals thwart hunters in the 2006 Sony Pictures movie Open Season.

Most giant beaver remains have been found in the American Midwest, including the first fossils from Ohio in 1837.

BENEFICIAL BEAVERS

The earliest beaver ancestors belonged to a group of small rodent-like mammals in the genus *Agnotocastor*, which existed in Europe, Asia, and North America about 30 million years ago. These animals were aquatic and had chisel-like teeth, but they are not considered to be true beavers. According to rare fossils found in Germany more than 100 years ago, the first modern beavers emerged about 12 million years ago. The additional discovery of 7-million-year-old beaver teeth in Oregon in 2011 has led researchers to infer that today's beavers remain similar to these later ancestors both in their appearance and in their role in the **ecosystem** as important habitat engineers.

By about 2 million years ago, most early beaver ancestors died off, leaving only a few species on the European and North American continents—most of them **evolving** to giant size. In Europe, *Trogontherium boisvillettei* weighed nearly 200 pounds (90.7 kg), and the largest rodents ever to have inhabited North America were 2 members of the genus *Castoroides*. They grew to 8 feet (2.4 m) in length and weighed up to 440 pounds (200 kg). Their gnawing

Although not a true beaver, the mountain beaver is so named because it gnaws bark and cuts off tree limbs.

Eurasian beavers typically build their dams to maintain streams rather than create ponds.

Beavers may make grunting sounds while working and will hiss or huff when they feel trapped.

front teeth were six inches (15.2 cm) long. The giant beavers disappeared from Earth about 10,000 years ago. Scientists believe early humans could have hunted them to extinction. Analysis of ice-age fossils has revealed that only the two species of small beavers we know today survived.

There were once as many as 100 million beavers in Europe and Asia and twice that many in North America, but by the early 20th century, both species had been hunted nearly to extinction. Beavers were hunted for their castoreum, which was used in perfumes and folk medicines, as well as for their meat and pelts. Legal protection and conservation efforts beginning in the 1960s, along with reintroduction programs, have since restored Eurasian beavers to most of their former habitats. Beaver populations are now stable; however, beavers across Europe and Asia are still threatened by illegal hunting, habitat loss, entanglement in fishing nets, water **contaminants**, and—particularly in northwestern Russia and Finland—competition with introduced North American beavers. Because of conservation efforts in the last 50 years, beavers in North America now number about 15 million.

Both Eurasian and North American beavers are considered **nuisance** animals in some places, particularly in agricultural regions. Damming and flooding can affect drainage systems and can damage crops, orchards, and **commercial** timber forests. In Canada, the U.S., and many European nations, when beavers become a problem, landowners may purchase a special permit to have the beavers killed. There are also many non-lethal methods of beaver control. To discourage beavers from settling in a particular area, landowners may wrap fencing or metal barriers around the tree trunks.

In addition to 4 sharp incisors, beavers have 16 other teeth they use for grinding and chewing food.

Unlike this typical lodge, the largest lodge ever found was 40 feet (12.2 m) across and 16 feet (4.9 m) high.

Another option involves the application to tree trunks of a chemical compound called thiram. This chemical gives off a strong odor that irritates beavers' noses. Running a pipe through a beaver dam to allow water to flow from one side to the other is a way of thwarting beavers' unwanted engineering. Beavers may clog culverts in ditches, restricting necessary water flow, but such problems can be addressed by installing mesh cages at the culvert openings. All these non-lethal methods of beaver management can be costly and difficult. Whenever possible, wildlife managers prefer to assist landowners in relocating beavers to more suitable habitats.

Many landowners welcome beavers on their property and are happy to adopt relocated beavers. In drier regions such as Texas and Wyoming, for example, many ranchers find that beaver dams increase the accumulation of underground water, which opens up watering holes for cattle and horses. Beaver ponds also improve the water quality of rivers by collecting and filtering pollutants and sediment from land runoff before these contaminants reach rivers. The wetlands that beavers create are also beneficial to wildlife, providing much-needed habitats for waterfowl, fish, frogs, and newts. Trees partially submerged when beaver ponds are created become waterlogged and die, providing vital nesting habitats for birds such as flycatchers, tree creepers, and owls. And in Europe, the canals that beavers create provide safe habitat for water voles—one of Europe's most endangered mammals.

Beavers provide other environmental benefits as well. As sediments are broken down by rainfall and erosion, they slowly settle into a beaver pond. When a pond fills with too much sediment, beavers will move to a different location up- or downstream to create a new pond. Without the maintenance of its dam, the abandoned pond

The cambial layer between a tree's bark and its inner wood is the mainstay of a beaver's diet.

The beaver's cardiac gland secretes extra digestive chemicals into the stomach to break down woody plant fiber.

Young aspens cannot thrive in shade, so beavers' thinning of mature trees keeps aspen forests healthy.

By trimming branches from standing willows, aspens, and cottonwoods, beavers help trees produce thicker growth.

eventually drains, and meadow grasses and wildflowers grow to cover it. This new area is called a beaver meadow, and it provides important habitat for birds, insects, and mammals such as foxes, skunks, and deer.

Sustainable beaver populations exist throughout Europe and North America today, though beavers are often reintroduced to places from which they had once been overhunted. Since the 1990s, the Oregon Department of Fish and Wildlife and the Fox Creek Land Trust have been restoring riparian zones throughout the state by planting willows and aspens and cleaning up wetlands in order to relocate beavers. In 2011, conservationists in Wales, where beavers had been extinct for 400 years, released beavers in a protected area in hopes of establishing a beaver colony. And in an effort to repopulate beavers in Mongolia and strengthen the Tuul River ecosystem, 7 pairs of beavers from Germany and 10 pairs from Russia were relocated to the Mongolian river in 2012. Only about 150 beavers remain in Mongolia, and about 700 exist in China. Despite strict laws protecting beavers, these animals are widely hunted in Asia.

Beavers are industrious and resilient animals, and while

drought and floods affect them more than predation, they primarily struggle against the pressures of human activity. As urbanization and agricultural expansion drive people ever deeper into wilderness areas, contact with beavers becomes inevitable, often leading to conflict over waterways and drainage systems. Understanding beavers' place in the global ecosystem and respecting their instinct to engineer and construct are necessary if we are to successfully share the world and its water with these inventive creatures.

Beavers make few vocal sounds, but whining is a form of communication that helps families affirm their bonds.

ANIMAL TALE: BEAVER'S CHALLENGE

Animals are an important part of the folklore of virtually every culture on Earth. This is especially true of beavers in North America. In this legend from the Tsimshian people of the Pacific Northwest, the beaver and the porcupine hold a competition to test their skills and ingenuity.

One summer day, Porcupine climbed a tall aspen tree to nibble on the leaves of its uppermost branches. He had no sooner begun to feast than the entire tree began to shake. "What is going on?" exclaimed Porcupine, clambering down the quaking tree.

At the base of the tree, Porcupine found Beaver furiously gnawing through the bark. "This is my tree!" Porcupine huffed.

"No, it's mine," Beaver argued, and with that he gave the tree a nudge, and it fell with a crash. Porcupine stomped off.

Beaver gripped the fallen tree in his jaws and dragged it toward the stream, where he was building a dam. At the stream, Beaver found Porcupine scraping liverworts off the rocks. Just as Porcupine was about to stuff a wad of the juicy plants into his mouth, Beaver knocked Porcupine into the water. "This is my stream," Beaver said.

"No, it's mine," Porcupine sputtered, dragging himself onto the bank.

"Go live somewhere else," Beaver said.

"You should go away," Porcupine replied.

Blue Jay had been listening to this argument from his aspen tree perch and flew down to offer some advice. "I suggest a contest," Blue Jay said. "Whichever of you fails must move away."

Porcupine thought for a while, and then he said to Beaver, "Only if you can reach the top of a tall aspen tree, may you stay."

Blue Jay shook his head, for he knew that Beaver, who could not climb, would never be able to reach the top of a tree.

Beaver said to Porcupine, "Only if you can cross from one bank of the stream to the other, may you stay."

Blue Jay sighed, for he knew that Porcupine, who could not swim, would never be able to cross the stream. Nevertheless, Beaver and Porcupine agreed to each other's challenge.

Soon summer turned to fall, and Beaver completed his dam. A pond formed and many of the aspen trees growing along the stream bank were now almost completely submerged in the deep pond. Beaver called out to Porcupine, "It is time to meet your challenge. Come see me reach the top of a tall aspen tree."

Porcupine hurried to the pond, expecting to see Beaver fail. Instead, Beaver swam over to a submerged tree and settled on its uppermost branch, which peeked above the water's surface. "There," said Beaver, "I am at the top of a tall tree, so I can stay."

"Fine," said Porcupine, angered at being tricked.

Soon fall turned to winter. "Now it is my turn," Porcupine called to Beaver. "I will meet your challenge by crossing the stream."

Beaver emerged from his lodge to watch Porcupine, expecting him to drown. Instead, Porcupine simply stepped across the patches of ice that covered the stream. "There," said Porcupine, "I crossed the stream, so I can stay."

"Fine," Beaver said, angry at this trickery, and he hurried back to his lodge to escape the cold winter wind.

To this day, Beaver and Porcupine continue to share the forest, but they still do not get along!

GLOSSARY

colonized – established settlements in a new land and exercised control over them

commercial – used for business and to gain a profit rather than for personal reasons

contaminants – non-natural substances that have a negative effect upon the environment or animals

cultures – particular groups in a society that share behaviors and characteristics that are accepted as normal by that group

dexterous – having skill or agility in using the hands or body to perform tasks

ecosystem – a community of organisms that live together in an environment

evolving – gradually developing into a new form

extinction – the act or process of becoming extinct; coming to an end or dying out

genetically – relating to genes, the basic physical units of heredity

gestation – the period of time it takes a baby to develop inside its mother's womb

glands – organs in a human or animal body that produce chemical substances used by other parts of the body

mammals – warm-blooded animals that have a backbone and hair or fur, give birth to live young, and produce milk to feed their young

mythology – a collection of myths, or popular, traditional beliefs or stories that explain how something came to be or that are associated with a person or object

nuisance – something annoying or harmful to people or the land

pelts – the skins of animals with the fur or wool still attached

satellite – a mechanical device launched into space; it may be designed to travel around Earth or toward other planets or the sun

semiaquatic – living partly on land and partly in water

sustainable – able to be renewed or kept functioning

weaned – made the young of a mammal accept food other than nursing milk

SELECTED BIBLIOGRAPHY

Beavers: Wetlands & Wildlife. "About Beavers." http://www.beaversww.org/beavers-and-wetlands/about-beavers.

Minnesota Zoo. "North American Beaver." http://www.mnzoo.com/animals/animals_beaver.asp.

Müller-Schwarze, Dietland. *The Beaver: Its Life and Impact.* Ithaca, N.Y.: Comstock Publishing Associates, 2011.

————, and Lixing Sun. *The Beaver: Natural History of a Wetlands Engineer.* Ithaca, N.Y.: Comstock Publishing Associates, 2003.

New Hampshire Public Television. NatureWorks. "Beaver – *Castor canadensis.*" http://www.nhptv.org/natureworks/beaver.htm.

Rue, Leonard Lee III. *Beavers.* Stillwater, Minn.: Voyageur Press, 2002.

Note: Every effort has been made to ensure that any websites listed above were active at the time of publication. However, because of the nature of the Internet, it is impossible to guarantee that these sites will remain active indefinitely or that their contents will not be altered.

Beavers engineer their surroundings in ways that ensure a variety of forest wildlife will enjoy valuable habitat.

INDEX